Tap into Sap

Contents

Features

Sticky, Sugary Sap

Sap is a mixture of water, sugar, and **minerals.** It moves along tubes in a plant's stem or trunk from the roots to the leaves. Some plants make a special sap that helps them heal if they are cut. The sap of many plants is sweet. Both people and animals like to tap into this sugary sap for a treat.

FAST FACTS

Long ago, the Mayans of Central America used the sap of the rubber tree to make shoes. They dipped their feet into bowls of rubber sap. After a few hours, the sap dried into perfectly-fitting rubber shoes.

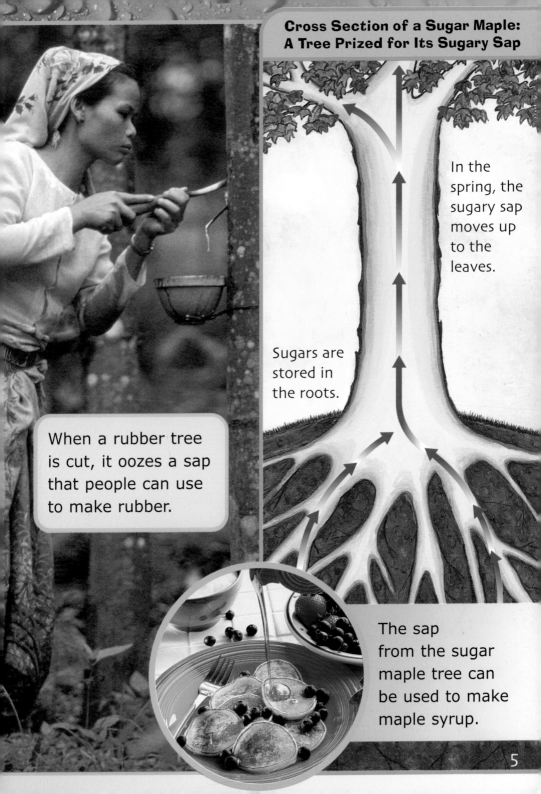

Cross Section of a Sugar Maple: A Tree Prized for Its Sugary Sap

In the spring, the sugary sap moves up to the leaves.

Sugars are stored in the roots.

When a rubber tree is cut, it oozes a sap that people can use to make rubber.

The sap from the sugar maple tree can be used to make maple syrup.

Drilling for Sap

Sapsuckers are birds that belong to the woodpecker family. After spending winter in the southern United States, they **migrate** north, looking for spring sap. Sapsuckers drill small round holes called wells into tree trunks with their strong beaks. They use their long tongues to lap the sticky sap.

Other birds and insects sneak in and share the sapsuckers' sugary food.

Sapsuckers nest in holes in trees. Besides eating sap, they eat the insects that come to feed on the sap.

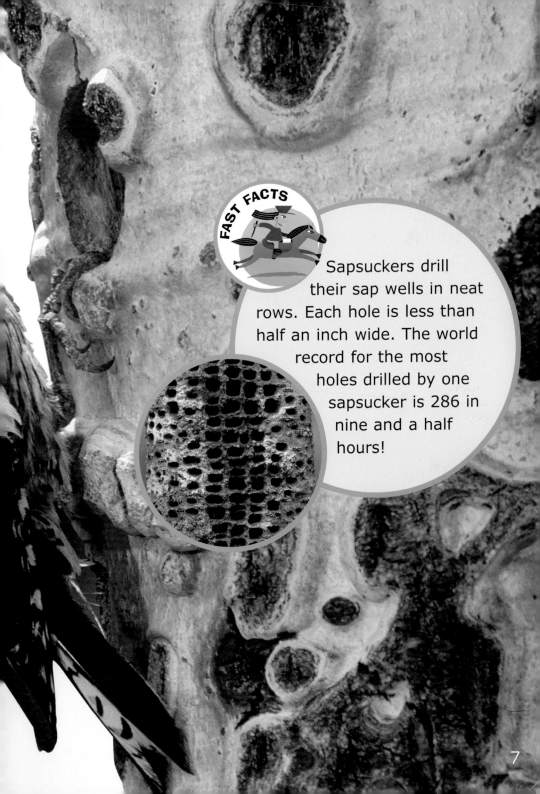

Sapsuckers drill their sap wells in neat rows. Each hole is less than half an inch wide. The world record for the most holes drilled by one sapsucker is 286 in nine and a half hours!

Butterflies and other insects also eat sap if they can find it. Butterflies suck up sap that has been left behind by animals. Other insects look for sap oozing from cut or injured trees.

Some honey ants store sap and nectar in their bodies. They look like tiny balloons and get so big that they cannot move. When there is little food, these ants will feed the colony from their stores.

Honey ants

These insects are sucking the sap of a Japanese oak tree.

TIME LINK

Sap of the Past

Over millions of years, tree sap hardens and turns into amber. Today, people find amber buried underground. Some of the amber contains insects that have been trapped in the sticky sap and preserved for millions of years.

Amber

Feasts in the Trees

Many animals that live in trees feast on sap. Squirrels, chipmunks, and porcupines lick sap from unguarded sap holes. Sugar gliders and flying squirrels leap for their sugary meals.

Sugar gliders and flying squirrels have special flaps of skin that help them leap from tree to tree. They can glide up to 100 yards at a time, searching for sap.

The kaka, a parrot in New Zealand, sometimes strips the bark off trees to reach the sap underneath.

Sugar glider

This sugar glider lives in Australia. It is **nocturnal.** Sap is an important part of its diet.

11

Glorious Gum

Some trees make a thick kind of sap called gum. Animals that eat this sap are called **gummivores**. The pygmy marmoset is a gummivore. It is the smallest monkey in the world. Pygmy marmosets eat fruit, leaves, and insects, but they spend most of their time chewing holes in trees, searching for gooey gum.

Gum is rich in **nutrients.** Pygmy marmosets give birth to twins twice a year, so they need plenty of nutrients.

Gum is often used to make glue. Gum is also used as a thickener in food such as ice cream and candy.

Gum glue

Ring-tailed lemurs get a lot of **vitamins** and other nutrients from tree gum.

13

Marvelous Maples

Sugar maple trees in Canada and the United States have a sweet, colorless sap. During the winter, the sap is stored in the trees' roots. In early spring when freezing nights are followed by warm days, the sap begins to flow up from the roots and through the trunk.

Native Americans were the first people to make maple sugar from sap. They ate maple sugar on fruit, vegetables, grains, and even fish.

Sugar maple tree

WORD BUILDER

Native Americans have different names for maple syrup and maple sugar. One name for maple sugar is *sinzibukwud*, which means "drawn, or taken, from the wood."

Native Americans made maple syrup and sugar by putting heated stones into the sap to cook it. As the stones cooled, they were replaced with hot stones to keep the sap boiling.

SITESEEING · PEOPLE & PLACES ·

Read a maple legend and learn about rubber.

Visit **www.rigbyinfoquest.com** for more about SAP.

Tree Tapping

Early American settlers learned from Native Americans how to tap into sugar maple trees. They carefully drilled holes into the tree trunks and then hammered tubes into the holes so the sap could flow into buckets. The sap was then poured into barrels and taken by horse-pulled wagons or sleds to sugarhouses for boiling.

1

Today, many sugarmakers harvest sap by running plastic tubes from holes in the trees directly into the sugarhouses. The sap is then boiled until sweet maple syrup is left. The syrup can be boiled and stirred to harden into sugar.

Sugaring Off

Much sap and a great deal of work is needed to make maple syrup. The water is boiled from the maple sap. This is called sugaring off. It takes 30–40 gallons of sap to make 1 gallon of maple syrup. People also use sap to make maple butter, candy, jelly, and other treats.

Many towns celebrate the sugaring season with sugaring off festivals. At these festivals, people often dress in old-time clothing and make maple syrup the old-time way.

Maple syrup comes in different shades of golden brown. The lighter shades have milder flavors and cost more to buy.

This woman is blowing bubbles from hot maple syrup to test if it is ready to be made into sugar.

19

Maple Muffins

TRY THIS!

Ingredients:

- 2 cups flour
- 3 teaspoons baking powder
- 1/2 teaspoon salt
- 2 tablespoons sugar
- 1/4 cup margarine
- 1 egg
- 3/4 cup maple syrup
- 1/4 cup milk

Equipment:

- 2 mixing bowls
- 1 measuring cup
- 1 set of measuring spoons
- 1 mixing spoon
- 1 spatula
- 1 muffin pan

Makes 12 muffins

Method

Step 1

Put the dry ingredients into a mixing bowl. Stir together.

Step 2

In another bowl, mix the margarine, egg, maple syrup, and milk.

Step 3

Pour the liquid ingredients into the dry ingredients and stir well.

Step 4

Grease and half-fill the muffin cups. Bake at 400°F for 10 minutes.

(Remember to get an adult to help you get the muffins in and out of the oven.)

Discussion Starters

1 People use the sap from rubber trees and the gum from gum-producing trees to make many things. What different uses of rubber and gum can you think of?

2 Native Americans were the first people to collect and eat the sap of the sugar maple tree. There are several legends explaining how they discovered this tasty treat. Try making up your own legend about the first time someone turned sap into syrup.

3 For people living in parts of Canada and the United States, the sugaring season is an important time of year. Many towns hold sugaring off festivals. Compare this with other planting or harvesting festivals that you know.